BOLD KIDS

Mardi Gras

A VARIETY OF FACTS
CHILDREN'S HOLIDAY BOOK

If you've ever visited New Orleans, you've likely seen the colorful parades and enthralling masks. But what do you really know about Mardi Gras and what makes it so unique?

Here are some facts about the festival's traditions, colors, and Krewes. Plus, don't forget about the King cakes! This is a fun-filled holiday for the whole family!

TRADITIONS

Mardi Gras tradition is celebrated with the king cake. This special dessert was named after the Three Kings who brought gifts to baby Jesus.

Some bakeries in New Orleans started inserting tiny baby figurines inside king cakes, and the lucky recipient would be considered the king for a day. Later, this idea was modified to avoid lawsuits. Now, it is an important part of Mardi Gras traditions.

MARDI
GRAS

The Zulus, the oldest African American krewe in New Orleans, holds a traditional parade. However, instead of throwing coconuts into the crowd, they hand out decorated coconuts to spectators.

Unlike today, coconuts handed out by the Zulus are not supermarket ones. Instead, they are covered in glitter and painted. Many spectators claim to have been injured during the parade. As a result, many people don't participate in the parade.

Traditionally, Mardi Gras celebrations include heavy drinking. In fact, heavy drinking has become synonymous with the French Quarter. The New Orleans Mardi Gras celebration is celebrated by locals of all heritages. In fact, the city's slogan, "Laissez les bons temps roule," came from these celebrations.

There are more than a hundred grand balls held in New Orleans during the Carnival season. Many of them are invitation-only, but some are open to the public. In addition, formal dresses and debutante introductions are a part of the festivities.

A traditional French celebration includes masquerade balls held by different families each weekend. Some of these festivities lasted for two months. The name Mardi Gras, which means "fat Tuesday," refers to the Tuesday before Ash Wednesday, when people used up all of their meat and dairy products.

Nowadays, the term refers to the whole period of celebrations. And because the Mardi Gras celebration is so popular, people all over the world celebrate it!

SIDEWALK
CLOSED
HERE

COLORS

In the history of Mardi Gras, there are many different colors. Purple, green, and gold are three of the most common colors seen during the holiday. The colors were chosen because they are rich and vibrant, and because they complement each other.

But what's the significance of these colors? Let's look at some of the symbols associated with these colors. This book will look at the meaning of these colors and their significance in the festival.

The colors of Mardi Gras were originally selected by the Rex Organization in 1872, when they were tasked with throwing a celebration for a Russian grand duke.

The Rex organization chose purple, gold, and green as the official colors of Mardi Gras, and the organization selected a new monarch each year known as the "King of Carnival." The krewe's official colors were purple, gold, and green.

The Mardi Gras colors reflect the many celebrations held throughout the year. These celebrations take place in many cities around the world and are celebrated before Lent.

If you're not able to attend Mardi Gras festivities, you can still celebrate the holiday by learning about the colors. Don't forget to enjoy King's Cake! And don't forget to wear your best green and gold attire!

In addition to wearing brightly colored clothing and masks during the parade, you can also dress in the colors of the festival. During the Mardi Gras season, you'll have the opportunity to enjoy the delicious food and drink of the city.

The food, music, and art all have the unique flavor of Mardi Gras. The colors also represent the freedom to enjoy life and socialize with people of different classes.

KREWES

There are several Krewes of Mardi Gra in New Orleans, each with their own tradition and flair. These groups throw Mardi Gras balls, ride on parade floats, and participate in social events all year long.

There are over 50 krewes in Southwest Louisiana alone, and they are organized into a large organization called the Krewe of Mardi Gras.

The parade is not organized solely to celebrate the grand duke of Kiev's visit, but the event added to the frolic and excitement. Local newspapers printed satirical letters to the royal colleagues Rex and Alexei, which was later published in the official Mardi Gras newspaper.

This event is also known as the Bourbon Street Awards show. At noon on Fat Tuesday, krewes roll down Bourbon Street with elaborate floats decorated with intricate art, colorful decorations, and flashing LED lights.

The krewes of Mardi Gras are an extension of New Orleans culture. Founded in the nineteenth century, these groups have become a cultural and social force.

Many of them have become household names, with the most famous being the Rex krewe, which has the title of "King of Carnival."

The Krewe of Vieux is considered to be the most irreverent of all. The krewe's costumes and floats are wildly outrageous, with sexual and political themes.

The Endymion krewe is one of the largest and most extravagant. Two years ago, the float featured Kevin Costner. Besides Costner, other notable celebrities who have led the parades have included Dan Aykroyd, John Goodman, and Chuck Norris.

KING CAKES

Before we start talking about king cakes as Mardi Gras facts, let's look at how the cake got its name. The term comes from the French tradition of eating rich foods prior to Lent, the forty days leading up to Easter, during which a fattened calf is slaughtered.

It's similar to the English tradition of eating pancakes, but instead of a king, the cake has a crown and three little figurines inside. King cakes also bear the names of the three wisemen who visited Jesus after his birth.

While the name is undoubtedly derived from the French, the origins of king cakes go back to the period when the French colonists first arrived in New Orleans.

These French settlers brought with them their own traditions, including Carnival and the King Cake, and later modified them to fit in with the New World. The history of the King Cake, and other Mardi Gras facts, can be learned from these interesting facts.